Coming Home

COMING HOME
a Collection

Sue Shellabarger Pettit

Sunrise Press
9700 Fair Oaks Blvd., Suite C
Fair Oaks, California   95628

COMING HOME
a Collection

Cover design by Jane Dimino

Copyright 1987 by Sue Shellabarger Pettit

Library of Congress
    catalog card number: 87-062047

ISBN: 0-9606896-7-2

I live with a man - Bill Pettit.
He has always searched for a better way.
He shares a journey of living and love.

To him
To my children - Ann
                      Daniel
                      Margaret
                      Mollie

And to all who have been looking for a better way -

I dedicate this book.

Table Of Contents

ACKNOWLEDGMENTS

I heard a man - George Pransky.
He talked about the World of Thought vs. the World of
Deeper Feelings.
He shared Hope.

I heard a man - Rick Suarez.
He talked about Psychology of Mind.
He shared Understanding.

I heard a man - Syd Banks.
He talked about Love, Wisdom and a
Higher Consciousness.
He shared Truth.

With deepest gratitude, I thank these people.

My life - therefore - my poems - have been influenced and enriched by the people who have shared with me - through their living examples, their seminars and their books.

With sincere appreciation I would like to share this information.

Banks, Syd. *Second Chance.* New York: Ballantine, 1987.

Nelsen, Jane. *Understanding.* Fair Oaks, CA: Sunrise Press, 1986.

Suarez, Rick, Mills, Roger & Stuart, Darlene. *Sanity, Insantiy & Common Sense.* New York: Fawcett Columbine, 1987.

Coming Home

*Coming home is about coming back to
myself and my own wisdom. It is about
finding that peaceful place within; a
place where I feel secure and full.*

*Coming home was written as a celebration
as I began to realize that the only thing
that takes me away from a peaceful life
is traveling in my own thoughts.
To come home I only needed to understand
what thought was and how I used it.*

*When I am home, the world is a
wondrous place.
To all who have searched -
WELCOME HOME!*

COMING HOME

Coming home to peace and quiet.
Coming home to feelings warm.
Coming home where there's a fullness,
where love in me is born.
Coming home's a simple journey,
takes no movement on my part.
Instead of listening to my thoughts,
I listen with
my heart.

LILLY'S LOOSE

Lilly is the operator
at the switchboard of my brain.
And when she starts reacting,
my life becomes insane.
She's supposed to be employed by me
and play a passive role.
But - anytime I'm insecure-
Lilly takes control.

Lilly's loose,
Lilly's loose,
Lilly's loose today!
Tell everyone around me
just to clear out of my way.
The things I say won't make much sense-
all COMMON SENSE is lost-
'Cause when Lilly's at the switchboard
my wires all get crossed.

Lilly is my own creation,
thought I needed her with me
To organize and then recall
all my life's history.
But she started taking liberty
with all my information.
And whenever she starts plugging in
I get a bad sensation.

Lilly's loose,
Lilly's loose,
Lilly's loose today.
Tell the world to hurry by
and stay out of my way.
I'm feeling very scattered-
I'm lost in my emotion.
Lilly's on a rampage
and she's causing a commotion.

She looks out through my eyeballs
and sees what I do see,
Then hooks up wires to my past-
she thinks she's helping me.
When I'm in a good mood
I can smile at her endeavor.
But when I'm in a bad mood
Lilly's boss, and is she clever.

Lilly's loose, Lilly's loose,
Lilly's loose today
Tell all my friends and relatives
to stay out of my way.
I don't give hugs and kisses
when I'm in this frame of mind.
And please don't take me seriously-
It'd be a waste of time.

LILLY'S LOOSE!

SHADOWDANCE

My thoughts are like the shadows that
  when young
    filled me with fright;
The monsters that surrounded me
'til Mom turned on the light.
When the light was off
    'twas scary;
with light on
    there was relief.
The world-
  it hadn't changed a bit;
  just thought changed-
my belief.

My thoughts create illusions
then a certain way I feel;
Happy or sad,
  scared or mad,
    yet none of it is real.
When thoughts begin their shadowdance
and peace from me is gone.
There is a light switch to my mind -
DEEPER FEELINGS turn it on.

THUNDERDROPS OR RAINDROPS

We were driving down a country road,
    my son, Daniel, and I.
As we drove the day got darker,
    gray clouds rolled across the sky.
Soon any sight of winter sun
    was lost out of our view.
And as the last ray disappeared,
    young Daniel's smile did too.

Great raindrops started splashing
    and they seemed to cause alarm
To the little boy beside me.
    He sat close and hugged my arm.
I looked down upon the little head
    he buried in my side.
I could feel him start to tremble
    and his eyes were open wide.

"Are those THUNDERDROPS?" he asked me.
    I had never heard that word.
Thunderdrops, he said, were raindrops
    seen before the thunder's heard.
Thunder was a scary thing to him.
    Its noise filled him with dread.
And when he saw the raindrops fall,
    scary thoughts raced in his head.

The more he thought his scary thoughts,
  the more he felt his fears.
We did not hear it thunder,
  yet his eyes filled up with tears.
He did not need the thunder now
  to rumble in the skies.
It was real to him already
  as his thoughts became his eyes.

We all have our own thunderdrops;
  a word
    a sound
      a phrase.
And when they come into our life
  we get lost in our own maze.
Like Dan, we see beyond our eyes
  and live in thought's illusion.
The emotions caught inside these thoughts
  then color our delusions.

How many times, I wonder,
  How many moments lost
By things we think might happen -
  our sanity the cost.
Thunderdrops are only raindrops
  wrapped inside a troubled thought.
When you understand the wrapping
  you're less likely to get caught.

GREEN, NOT BLUE

I was out for a walk
when I happened to meet
the woman next door -
she was new on our street.
She nodded her head,
I returned her a smile.
And I thought-
She seems nice.
We've a similar style.

The next day we met
I took over some flowers.
We hit it off well.
We talked several hours.
She told me of her life.
I told her of mine.
And I thought -
I do like her.
This new neighbor's fine.

Then one day in the yard-
it is shocking but true-
this new friend of mine
called my green grass blue.
She kept calling green blue
'til I got so upset
And I thought -
I don't like her.
I'm sorry we met.

In everything else
we had seen eye to eye;
from the red of the rose
to the blue of the sky.
Now she disagreed firmly
with no hesitation.
And I thought-
I am right
and I'll get validation!

I called over Marie,
a real long time friend.
I just had to give
this discussion an end.
"Marie," I said, "Tell her
that this grass is green!"
And I thought-
What a neighbor-
to make such a scene.

Marie looked at it closely,
examined its hue.
She saw lots of my green-
not a hint of her blue.
So I nodded my head
and I folded my arms.
And I thought-
Whew, I'm right.
There's no cause for alarm.

But my neighbor just smiled
and she said, "It's ok.
I just happen to see
your green grass my own way."
She wouldn't admit
that she saw green all wrong.
So I thought-
With her outlook
our friend days are gone.

I stopped going over
to visit with her.
What I saw and she saw
just didn't concur.
We couldn't be friends
'cause we didn't agree.
For I thought-
All my friends
have to see just like me.

As the years passed me by
lots of friends passed by too
Over matters important-
like green versus blue.
Just one little difference
could lead to a fight.
'Cause I thought-
In my world,
    there is only one right.

I'm much wiser now.
I don't see the same way.
My heart
*   not my eyes*
looks upon each new day.
When I look from my heart,
friends are blessings to me.
Without thought-
There is room
for all colors,
I see.

THE SEARCH

From all the articles I read
I got this notion in my head.
"I have to find myself," I said.
And started on my search.

This search "for me" has taken years.
It's cost me friendships, time and tears.
I've searched through all my pain and fears.
"Where did I lose myself?"

The search was my reality.
How could I stop 'til I found me?
I longed for my identity
But you know what I discovered?

The searching was inside of me,
Comparing me with all I'd see,
Fueled by my insecurity
And triggered by my thoughts.

The search was just inside my brain.
It took such effort, toil and strain.
It often drove me quite insane
This looking for myself.

So, I stopped the search and lived the day
And I found myself along the way.
I let my feelings lead today.
Life's much more simple now.

I've cleared self-help books off my shelf.
I've started listening to myself.
I've found my reservoir of wealth
Of common sense inside.

The search for me is done today!
I never really went astray.
I'm throwing troubled thoughts away -
Without them - - - Here I am.

ANNIE - IN GRATITUDE

What is this child I watch tonight
as she lay sleeping soundly;
An independent spirit bright
or a life that's bound to me?
What do I ask of this young child?
Will it change from year to year?

Oh, let me just be grateful,
for each day that she is near.

In gratitude
where I feel full
There'll be no need to judge.
There'll never be a silence long
from which we need to budge;
There'll never be the wasted days
that we can ne'er recapture.
In gratitude
we both will know
I'm just so glad I have her.

TENSION?

Thoughts create all our "bad" feelings.
If we don't know of this fact
We begin to treat our feelings real
and to them we react.
Then soon it's not the task at hand
that's getting our attention;
Instead we wrestle with each thought
and THAT creates our tension.

QUIET

Quiet,
    when I define it,
        means a total lack of sound;
A moment without movement,
A stillness all around.

Quiet,
    when I feel it,
        has a different quality.
It's a full and peaceful presence
Permeating all of me.

WHEN A WONDER

Something ageless
   Something timeless
      Something measureless fills me
When a wonder
   In my very ordinary life I see.
There's a meeting
   In that moment
      Past with present is imbued.
It surrounds me
   And profounds me
      With a sense of gratitude.
In that moment I have vision
   Far beyond what I can see
Of my commonness with others,
   All the world is part of me.

MULTIPLICATION

I looked up and I watched her
  slowly come in the front door.
She looked so very tired and hot -
  dropped books upon the floor.
After seven hours of school, she sighed,
  there was more work in her day.
There was spelling and science and math to do,
  to complete before her play.

She sat down to do her homework.
  First was math - page ninety two.
And her stomach did a flip flop -
  there was so much work to do.
Now, it's true the problems numbered
  only twenty, but you see
Her thoughts raced 'round; they got her down;
  she felt the urge to flee.

Her thoughts were weary burdens:
  some about her day at school;
And of the heat that was around her,
  how she wished she had a pool;
The girl that talked to her in math
  and "made" her fall behind;
Of the friends she'd won and lost - that day -
  no the thoughts weren't very kind.

She had only twenty problems.
Lost in thought she saw lots more.
As she counted and recounted them
she slid down on the floor.
She moaned and groaned and thought some more,
remembering each past error.
And when she faced the page again
twenty problems brought her terror.

They'd been added to and multiplied!
She felt so overwrought.
The fear she felt, the overwhelm,
seemed more real than just a thought.
She sat and stared and wiggled,
then to add to her dismay,
She thought - I'll never finish this.
I'll never get to play.

She looked at me, perhaps to see
*   if she had a friend that day.*
It used to be, in my sympathy
*   I'd get lost in her dismay.*
She would moan about her homework.
*   I would nag 'til it was done.*
Then I'd wonder why so many days
*   would pass between our fun.*

Now I'm seeing this much differently
*   and the help I have to offer*
Is to point her to a peaceful place -
*   that's safe - and that's within her.*

I can't help her when I'm adding to
*   the turmoil that she feels.*
I can only help to teach her
*   that these feelings are not real:*
That it's not the twenty problems
*   that will cause her such distress*
But the weight of all the other thoughts
*   that make math seem a mess.*

Knowing this, I smile upon her
*   for I know it is in thought*
All about the past and future
*   and "what ifs" that she's been caught.*
It has hidden sunshine from her heart,
*   good feelings from her day.*
And when she stops this flow of thought
*   these woes will go away.*

ILLUSION'S INTRUSIONS

To do just what we're doing -
that's the thing we've got to learn.
To enjoy each moment's business -
work and play - each in its turn.
And the only thing that keeps us
from enjoying what we do
Is believing those bad feelings
that our thoughts can give life to.

Yes - our thoughts create bad feelings
but these feelings are illusions.
To know
and understand this
will start stopping their intrusions.

ONE SMILE

One smile in a world of frowns
Elevates the depth of downs.

One smile from deep within
Dulls the sharpness of chagrin.

One smile feeling good to wear
Pours compassion into care.

One smile on the smiler's face
Illuminates a peaceful place.

One smile to another's eyes
Unlocks hope - and spirits rise.

IT COULD HAVE BEEN FUNNY

It could have been funny -
what happened last night.
It could have been funny -
she looked quite a sight.
When a Halloween "glow stick"
popped open and dribbled,
Its contents of green glow
upon her did scribble.

It could have been funny.
We could have all laughed.
But I was too tired
and my good mood had passed.

As I stared with chagrin
at the mess she had made,
I knew I'd explode
if around her I stayed.
So instead of some laughter,
sweet moments to share,
I got mad and I left her
with a cold, scolding stare.

Now the mess is cleaned up
     and my tiredness is gone.
And I "see" a new sight
     in the new morning dawn.

How different, how pleasant,
     how fun it would be
To turn back the clock -
     in this mood I would see
The child that I love
     GLOWING GREEN in the night.
And I'd laugh with her,
     sharing her startled delight.
Then we'd wash it all off
     and she'd climb into bed
And I'd tuck her in gently
     and kiss her forehead.

Yes,
It could have been funny.
     Now it's clear to me!
My moods really "change"
     What I feel, what I see.

THE LAST ILLUSION

The last illusion:

The one last thing
I think I need
to end confusion.

The last illusion:

Holds promises
of all I want
in such profusion.

The last illusion:

A fickle thing
that changes with
thought's convolution.

The last illusion.

COMPASSION'S RIPPLE

Whenever there's a person
    with compassion in their smile
All those they meet are mellowed
    and this feeling stays a while.
Then all the people that they meet
    receive a softness too.
And on it goes, this rippling
    to everyone in view.
It doesn't matter what you do
    or who you meet each day.
The peace you find within yourself
    will touch the world this way.

WORKING ON RELATIONSHIPS

I've worked on my relationship -
  for years - it seems to me.
The harder that I work on it
  the more flaws I do see.
It's when I weary of the working -
  and give up - that's when I know,
All the joys of being with him.
  And the feelings of love grow.

HIS HOME

"What's homesick, mommy?" my child asked me,
　　in a voice both soft and serious.
At eight years old, this word to him
　　had sounded quite mysterious.
I said "It's when you miss your home
　　and wish that you were there,
Back home with all the ones you love,
　　with all the ones who care.

"I was homesick once." he said to me
　　with sober eyes of blue.
"But I was home and YOU were gone ----
　　I was homesick for you!"

For a moment I was speechless
　　as his insight captured me.
Then I smiled at him and we both laughed.
　　It was so plain to see.

To him "home" was not a place at all
　　with floors and doors and ceilings.
His home was a place inside his heart -
　　a place of deeper feelings.
His home was love, his home was joy -
　　a peacefulness within.
And that night as we laughed
　　I could tell he was home -
　　　　just looking at his grin.

HOW LONG IS AN HOUR?

"How long is an hour, Mom?"
my children asked one night
As I was tucking them in bed
and turning out the light.
They listened very closely
as I attempted to convey
That hours change - some long, some short,
when THOUGHT comes into play.

I said an hour's sixty minutes -
That fact everybody knows -
It's two Laverne and Shirleys -
It's two Bill Cosby shows -
It's the time it takes the big hand
to go from 12 to 12 -
But to understand time's fickleness
one more factor we must delve.

An hour - when you're smiling
and playing with a friend
Seems like a very short time -
too soon it's at its end.
The hour that seems long
when your friend is gone away
Is the hour that seems short
when he comes back to play.

See,
It's not the hour on the clock
   that changes its duration.
It's what goes on INSIDE YOUR HEAD
   that yields time's fluctuation.

BABY MARGARET

Baby, dear Baby, tell me what do you see?
Do you see an angel standing by me?
You look so hard past me with those great dark eyes.
You are just three weeks old, yet your look is so wise.

Sometimes when outside, your eyes turn to the sky
And you seem to be listening and looking up high.
What do you hear, Baby? What do you see?
I raise my eyes up, but it's just sky to me.

It's as if you're a part of a whole other time
And slowly you learn to become part of mine.
Each day you let go of some part of that place
As you join in our life. It reflects on your face.

I welcome each moment you spend close with me.
You coo, and you smile, and as you start to see
All the people around you with love in their eyes.
Then we win you to us.
    You look down from the skies.

Yet I can't help reflecting each day as you grow,
What wonders you've looked at -- what secrets you know.
And I sense that each day -- each new thing that you learn
Requires you to give up these things in their turn.

I hold you so quiet and watch you and wonder
Do I somehow remember my first days, I ponder.
And is all of my traveling and learning new ways
Just to try to recapture the peace of those days?

For peaceful you are, while awake or asleep
And this feeling's contagious to all that you meet.
In this powerful smallness of life at its start
There's a message of hope and of love for each heart.

WHAT A DAY!

I woke up this morning
*   and looked all around.*
The house was so quiet,
*   there wasn't a sound.*
There was no warning
*   in the still morning air*
Of the "bad mood" inside me,
*   but it was there!*

It started to surface
*   as I got out of bed.*
It crept from my toes
*   and it filled my whole head.*
It swirled all around me
*   as real as could be*
'Til it colored and blurred
*   everything I could see.*

Now the tricky thing is,
*   this bad mood seemed so real*
That my whole life set-up
*   seemed like a bad deal.*
I lost common sense
*   and began to believe*
There was nothing worthwhile
*   in my life to retrieve.*

I walked 'round the house
*   with a scowl on my face.*
My eyes zeroed in
*   on each thing out of place.*
I thought to myself
*   just how nice life would be*
If I lived all alone
*   and just took care of me!*

No toilets left unflushed,
*   no underwear piles,*
No fingerprint smudges
*   on white bathroom tiles,*
No gum in the laundry,
*   no more spilled juice,*
No worry, no guilt, --
*   ah, but what's the use.*

'Cause I don't live alone,
*   I have kids and a mate.*
And they seem to know
*   all the things that I hate.*
Today, in this mood,
*   I was sure of their aim*
To break all my spirit,
*   and drive me insane.*

I gazed at their rooms.
What a mess! What a zoo!
They undo in just seconds
all the work that I do.
They live in this house,
but they never see
Even one single thing
they could do to help me.

Nooo! I'm just their mom,
the lady at home
Who washes their clothes
and answers the phone,
Who cooks and irons
and cleans up the dishes,
The one they get mad
at for unfulfilled wishes.

I recalled all the times
I had yelled at the kids,
And I spent the whole day
feeling bad that I did,
And then I got mad
'cause "they" made me feel guilty.
And the cycle continued
to churn round inside me.

The kids both get home --
*   here comes dirt and loud noise*
And they argue and fight
*   over each other's toys.*
They moan over homework,
*   first spelling, then math.*
And we struggle again when
*   it's time for their bath.*

They've been home just three hours,
*   it seems like all day.*
I am needing a rest,
*   they are wanting to play.*
Every moment of time
*   seems like a big struggle*
As my "want" and my "need"
*   and my "should" thoughts I juggle.*

By the time Bill gets home,
*   I've had over eight hours*
To give this bad mood
*   some incredible powers.*
His smile looks just
*   like a glower to me.*
No longer a man,
*   but a monster I see.*

I keep meeting bad feelings
    the whole day through.
I am miserable,
    but I have no clue
That the mood I am in
    has colored the way
That I see everything --
    What a day! What a day!

WHAT A DAY - ANY DAY

What a day - anyday -
*   has to offer to me*
Depends on the mood
*   that I'm in, I can see.*
I have found that a bad mood
*   can change very quick*
'Cause the walls that surround it
*   are just a thought thick.*

A thought thick - a bad mood
*   is just a thick thought*
That I let weigh me down
*   and that makes me feel caught.*
A thought thick, one thought through,
*   just an instant away*
Is a feeling that freshens
*   and brightens each day.*

What a day - anyday -
*   has to offer to me*
Is my choice - when I know
*   that thoughts change what I see.*
So a day full of love
*   and good feelings I choose.*
And you know where I find this?
*   Inside Gratitude.*

WHAT A DAY - IN GRATITUDE

In the quiet of the morning,
    just before the dawn
I look around the stillness,
    and sigh a little yawn.
It's before the family gets up -
    before the breakfast rush.
I embrace the day awaiting -
    just beyond the morning hush.

It's funny how a good mood makes
    everything look bright.
It spreads a sunny color onto
    everything in sight.
It reaches out to all my life
    and lends a peaceful glow.
It fills me up - 'til I'm surprised -
    at all the things I know.

It's a day like any other.
    Nothing special planned to do.
Yet my mood is very sunny,
    all seems pleasant in my view.
And I realize as I sit there -
    all the GRATITUDE I feel.
It's another day for living
    and each moment's life is real.

As I walk around the house,
everything I see
Reminds me of the ones I love
who share this home with me.
Yea, it looks a little messy -
remnants of the night before
And the evening we spent quietly,
are resting on the floor.

There are Danny's worn out sneakers.
Oh, how many steps they've run.
And Annie's favorite jacket,
faded, worn, with hem undone.
I pick up some books and papers
and the kid's construction set
And all my other daily chores
will fill my day, and yet ---

It's a day that's very special.
I am carried by my mood.
Today my jobs - a Mom, a Wife -
fill me with gratitude.
True, they may not notice all I do,
but I thank the stars above
For all the time I share with them.
My sustenance is love.

Kids have been to school three hours,
    yet right now it seems all day.
It suddenly feels quiet.
    Guess I miss their sounds of play.
When they're home the world is chaos -
    sudden smiles, then sudden tears.
Yet that chaos is a treasure
    as my days flow into years.

Bill comes home. I smile, inside and out.
    A simple man I see,
Who shares these years
    of growing up of family with me.
With all of us together
    as the day begins to end
I look upon each one of them
    and see a special friend.

THE PERFECT HOUSE --
WHICH RHYMES WITH SPOUSE

I'd been hunting for a house all day
  and nothing seemed quite right.
Then I happened on my dream house,
  much to my delight.
As I moved from room to room,
  I could feel this house my home.
And once I settled into it,
  I knew I'd never roam.
It had everything I wanted
  and I smiled 'cause I could see
Special dreams that I had wished for
  would become reality.
It was in such good condition -
  not a thing I'd have to change.
Just move in and enjoy it.
  Peace and happiness would reign.

Three months later I sat looking
    at the room that I was in.
As I sat I started thinking
    "Gee, the carpets worn and thin.
And the walls could use a coat of paint -
    cream or maybe white,
That would make the room look larger
    and give it added light."
There was not a thing I did not change
    as I sat contemplating.
My dream house became a drab house
    needing much redecorating.
I no longer saw the things I had,
    just all that I must do.
Happiness is gone, I thought,
    'til all the work is through.
After thirteen years I moved out,
    couldn't stand it anymore.
With all the constant work to do,
    the house was one big chore.
I cursed the house for changing -
    though it really was the same.
But through the years - I lost my dream
    and I thought it was to blame.

Looking back - it all seems silly,
    can't believe I didn't see
That what made that house my dream house
    was a feeling inside me.
When I listened to that feeling
    I just knew the house was right.
It was when I listened to my thoughts,
    that the house became a fright.
So I went back to that same house
    dropping thoughts and expectations.
As I looked through love - I saw again
    my dream - a revelation.
So don't give up on your dream house
    when it seems a little worn.
Just go back and find the feeling -
    deep inside - where dreams are born.

WE WALKED TO THE ZOO
ALL TOGETHER
ALONE

A STORY ABOUT SEPARATE REALITIES

To understand separate realities is like finding a bridge that lets all meet at a place that is beyond thoughts - above differences. It is here - in the moment - where warmth, gratitude and compassion fill the spirit.

We walked to the zoo,
*   all together, alone.*
There was me and my mother
*   and my sister Sloan.*
We walked the same paths
*   side by side, hand in hand*
But we could have been walking
*   in three different lands.*

Mom loves to walk,
*   she has long legs you see,*
But for each step she takes
*   I have to take three.*
I love the zoo - but oh -
*   I hate to walk*
And Sloan, she's sixteen -
*   mostly she loves to talk.*

Sloan and my Mom
*   talk the whole time we go.*
They are so high above me
*   so I never know*
what they speak of or look at
*   because I can't see.*
So most times when "we" walk -
*   I'm just walking with me.*

WE STOPPED BY THE MONKEYS

The monkeys were chattering
loudly and free.
I started to chatter
but my Mom stopped me.
They swing by their tails!
I wish I had one.
I climbed up the fence,
but then Sloan stopped that fun.
They were graceful and quick
and funny to look at.
I couldn't act like them
and so I just sat
And pretended to climb
and chatter and swing
'Til Mom called and I saw,
I was still me, Darlene.

And Sloan, sister Sloan,
   just kept talking and talking.
Why, she didn't notice
   that we had stopped walking.
She didn't see monkeys
   or trees in her gaze --
She was too lost
   in her personal maze.
She'd noticed a pimple
   this morning, it seems,
And felt that it surely
   would end all her dreams.
Especially if one
   of her friends saw her face!
And she lived in this fear
   as we walked place to place.

Mom looked at the cages
*   and started to frown.*
She saw MILLIONS of monkeys
*   all running around.*
She hated loud noises.
*   She hated disorder.*
Her Mama had told her
*   that these were bad for her.*
"Please, Darlene! Please!
*   Stop that chattering sound.*
With all this confusion
*   my head starts to pound.*
I've had a hard day
*   and I want peace and quiet.*
Let's walk down that way
*   and leave all this riot."*

WE STOPPED BY THE LION

The lion was white!
 Can you believe that?
And it lay very still
 like a great stone cat.
It was sprawled on the grass
 and it opened its eyes
And it stared back at us
 as his tail swished off flies.
I climbed up a railing
 so I could be tall
But Mom pulled me down -
 she told me I'd fall.
So I lay on the grass
 and pretended to be
That lion who looked
 so peaceful to me.

Sloan was still talking,
*   and talking, and talking.*
But this time she noticed
*   that we had stopped walking.*
As she looked with her eyes
*   on the lion this day*
She just thought of herself
*   and this got in her way.*
So - instead of a lion
*   in peaceful repose*
She saw only a pimple -
*   great big - on her nose.*
Then she covered her face
*   and looked down on the ground.*
She saw nothing we passed
*   as her thoughts raced around.*

Mom thought that the lion looked
  peaceful, serene.
The grass that it lay on looked
  so cool and clean.
She wished she could rest,
  find that peacefulness too,
But she felt very nervous
  today at the zoo.
Whatever, she thinks,
  gets into that child
To chatter and climb
  and race so wild?
The next time I think
  I will walk all alone.
Or maybe I won't walk
  we'll all just stay home.

WE STOPPED BY THE TURTLES

The turtles were great big,
*   and clumpy, and slow.*
They bobble their heads
*   back and forth as they go,*
If I were a turtle
*   I'd walk slow - this way.*
I'd draw in my head
*   at the end of the day.*
I'd squish mud, just like this,
*   eat mosquitoes, and then*
Ah! Oh! Here Mom comes
*   taking my hand again.*
So I walk by my Mom
*   in slow motion and dream*
That I live in a great big
*   hard shell that is green.*

Still Sloan kept on talking
but we never heard.
The sound was so constant
the words so absurd.
She could have been home
or at school or a game.
The surroundings could differ,
her concerns were the same.
And yet, as she watched
the great turtle's slow pace
Her mutterings stopped,
worried lines left her face.
Their stillness and quiet
made room for her smile
As she lived in the world -
not her thoughts - for awhile.

Mom looked at the turtles
　　so heavy and slow.
"They look like I feel,"
　　she said very low.
But they are protected
　　so well all around
And I'm always so scared,
　　she thought with a frown.
I'm scared for myself
　　and my children, it seems
So scared and so guarded -
　　all I do is scream.
Then she laughed at herself.
　　"Can life be that bad -
To lose all the joy
　　and always feel sad?"

We all slowly walked
to the bridge at the zoo.
It was very high up,
everything was in view.
I could see without climbing
and Sloan stopped her talking.
We all sat on a big bench
to rest from our walking.

As we looked at
     animal cages from here;
Mom felt us close -
     and she lost all her fear.
She began to relax
     and the next thing she knew,
She was ever so glad to be
     here at the zoo.

I was just me,
     Darlene, almost five,
Glad to have Mom
     and sis by my side.
I was glad to be high,
     I could see everyplace.
I was glad to see Mom
     with a smile on her face.

Sloan sat with her arms
     around me and Mom.
Her pimple forgotten -
     she seemed very calm.
She let go of the thoughts
     that had plagued her all day,
She looked out on the world -
     and the world looked OK.

We'd walked through the zoo
*   all together, and yet*
In a way, on this bridge,
*   it was like we'd just met.*
Our three lands converged
*   and we shared for a while*
Our laughter and love -
*   each in our own style.*

It happens that way
*   and I love when it does.*
I always feel grateful
*   to feel so much love.*

Now - When I was little -
  say two or three -
My Mom would often
  discover me
Snuggling in her
  worn out chair
'Cause I was so sure
  her love was there.
That's where she held me,
  late at night
When I'd wake up
  and cry with fright.
I felt so safe -
  she cuddled me.
So I was sure that's
  where love would be.

But now I know
  that that's not true.
Love's always around -
  in me and in you.
And knowing this -
  I find it more.
(I knew it wasn't
  the chair - at four)

So in all that I do
and all that I say
I look for these feelings
in my own way.

And there it was -
just as real as could be -
As we sat on the bridge,
Mom, sis and me.

Yes, today on the bridge
   I felt it too.
The feelings so big -
   oh, they make me feel new.
We seemed far away
   from the things we had passed
And the thoughts they had triggered
   for each didn't last.

Without separate thoughts,
   and our own separate worlds
We enjoyed what we were -
   a mom and two girls.

The path we had walked
   I could look at and see,
Felt very different
   to Mom, sis and me.
We each told our tale
   of "our" walk through the zoo
And they were soooo different -
   we laughed - wouldn't you?

It was getting late
  and we had to go.
Where the afternoon went
  I'll never know.
As we repassed the cages,
  one by one,
We giggled and laughed
  and had such fun.
It all looked so different -
  and I thought with a grin
It always is - when
  these feelings come in.

None of us thought,
   or idly talked.
We just felt the sun
   and each other and walked.
No, not much was said
   as we walked back home;
As we walked home together,
      alone,
         not alone.

MY CHILDREN'S CORNER

AN EXPLANATION OF SEPARATE REALITIES
by Ann Pettit
11 years old

Different realities are when you see something
   and another person sees the same thing -
   but in a different way.
You yell at that person
   and argue with that person
because you think you are right
   and the other person is wrong.
And that person thinks she is right
   and you are wrong.

Bill likes math and Tom does not like math,
   but Tom likes English.
Bill does not like English.
That is what different realities are.

TINY AND SMALL
by Daniel Pettit
9 years old

I thought I'd like to be tiny.
I'd go into a lemon and probably be limey
If you were small
You might fit in the wall.
Both would be fun
But the day is done.

And I can't make some rhymes
for these last two lines.
So I'll just have to say
Goodby.